PUFFIN BOOKS
HAVE YOU MET THE ANGLO-INDIANS?

Anastasia Damani is an illustrator-turned-author, musician and theatre lover. When she's not donning one of these hats, she likes curling up with a warm cup of tea. After completing her graduation from Symbiosis Institute of Design, Pune with a degree in communication design, she began her journey in her hometown, Kolkata, and now lives in København (Copenhagen). Anastasia enjoys writing and illustrating across mediums with children's books as her first love. Through her work, she strives to promote love, confidence, respect and responsibility in children.

ADVANCE PRAISE FOR THE BOOK

'What a beautiful window into the world of lesser-known communities in India'—Ruskin Bond

For
Didima, Dadi and Shyamadida

Have you met the anglo-indians?

(Culture • Customs • Community)

written + illustrated by

Anastasia Damani

PUFFIN BOOKS

An imprint of Penguin Random House

PUFFIN BOOKS

USA | Canada | UK | Ireland | Australia
New Zealand | India | South Africa | China

Puffin Books is part of the Penguin Random House group of companies
whose addresses can be found at global.penguinrandomhouse.com

Published by Penguin Random House India Pvt. Ltd
7th Floor, Infinity Tower C, DLF Cyber City,
Gurgaon 122 002, Haryana, India

First published in Puffin Books by Penguin Random House India 2021

Text and illustrations copyright © Anastasia Damani 2021

ISBN 9780143451662

Typeset in Montserrat
Printed at Aarvee Promotions, India

www.penguin.co.in

introduction

Meeting new people can be exciting! Especially people who are different from us. This helps us open our hearts and minds to new cultures.

Having grown up in an Indo-European family, in the cosmopolitan heart of Kolkata, I have had the joy of being exposed to various cultures.

Respect and appreciation for the diversity in communities, food, language, religion and attire does not necessarily come naturally. Taking the time to broaden our horizons ensures that we not only learn about these differences but also learn to love them.

The best way to do this is to make new friends—it could be a neighbour, a classmate or perhaps even a character in a book.

Meet Aunty Joyce and Uncle
Charlie Lovedale. They have two
wonderful children, Rosie and
Leslie, and a third child who's
rather fluffy, Penny-the-Pom,
a Pomeranian.

The Lovedales are
anglo-
indians.

After the British left India in 1947, many British families decided to stay back and make India their new home. The Lovedales are one such family.

They are known as Anglo-Indians because their families are of both British and Indian descent.

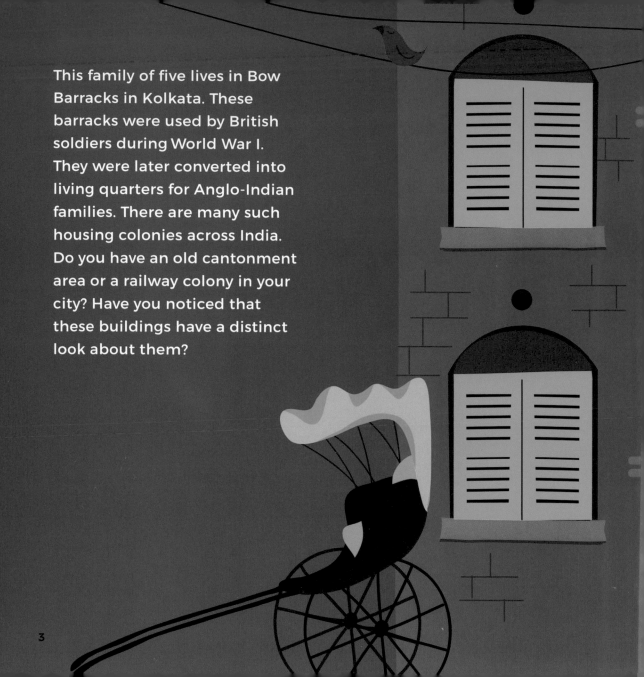

This family of five lives in Bow Barracks in Kolkata. These barracks were used by British soldiers during World War I. They were later converted into living quarters for Anglo-Indian families. There are many such housing colonies across India. Do you have an old cantonment area or a railway colony in your city? Have you noticed that these buildings have a distinct look about them?

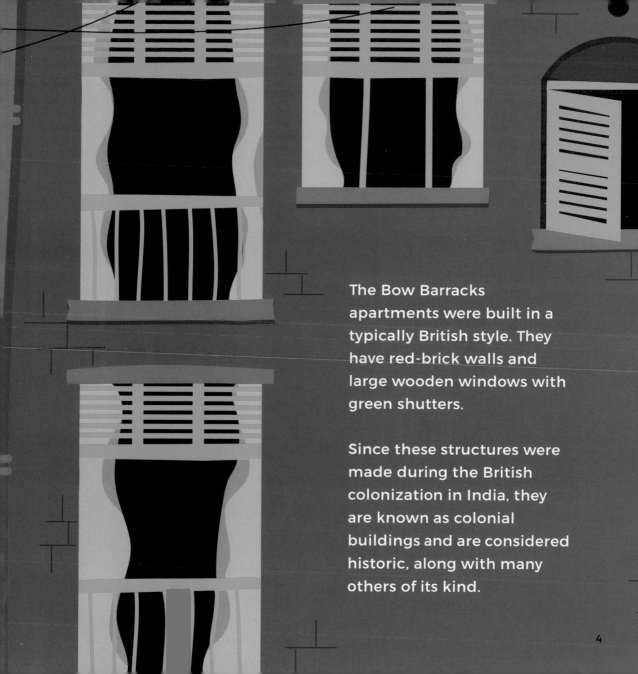

The Bow Barracks apartments were built in a typically British style. They have red-brick walls and large wooden windows with green shutters.

Since these structures were made during the British colonization in India, they are known as colonial buildings and are considered historic, along with many others of its kind.

4

Let's go on an

architecture adventure

to find colonial buildings around you. The style in which they were built is known as Indo-Gothic.

Some of their unique features are large arches, elegant pillars, majestic domes and towering spires. Perhaps it's a church, a railway station or a mansion. How many can you list?

Aunty Joyce is a music teacher at The Bishop's School, where Leslie and Rosie study.

When the British ruled India, they set up some of the first English-medium schools and colleges in our country. As a result, the people that taught and worked at these institutes were primarily British or Irish. However, when most of them left India after 1947, a few nuns and priests stayed back to continue running these schools and colleges. The Anglo-Indians were able to easily join them because their mother tongue was English.

Aunty Joyce teaches schoolchildren old Irish and English folk songs and rhymes. These songs were built around the theme of everyday life at the time. Some of them have hidden meanings and messages.

Here's the music and lyrics to a folk song. It can be sung as a duet, so find a partner to sing or recite along with you. Switch roles, use props and music, be dramatic, but most of all, have fun!

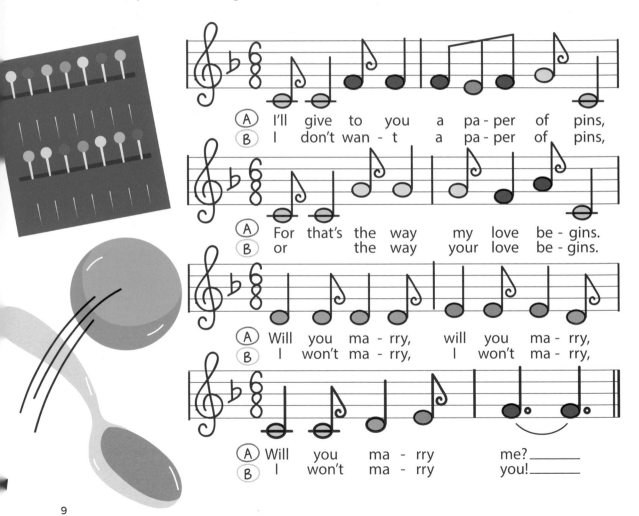

(A) I'll give to you a pa - per of pins,
(B) I don't wan - t a pa - per of pins,

(A) For that's the way my love be - gins.
(B) or the way your love be - gins.

(A) Will you ma - rry, will you ma - rry,
(B) I won't ma - rry, I won't ma - rry,

(A) Will you ma - rry me?_____
(B) I won't ma - rry you!_____

(A) I'll give to you a silver spoon,
To feed the baby in
the afternoon,
If you marry, if you marry,
if you marry me!

(B) I don't want a silver spoon,
To feed the baby in
the afternoon,
I won't marry, I won't marry,
I won't marry you!

(A) I'll give to you a golden ball,
To bounce from the kitchen
to the hall,
If you marry, if you marry,
if you marry me!

(B) I don't want a golden ball,
To bounce from the kitchen
to the hall,
I won't marry, I won't marry,
I won't marry you!

(A) I'll give to you the key to my chest,
And all the money that
I possess,
If you marry, if you marry,
if you marry me!

(B) I accept the key to your chest,
And all the money that
you possess,
I will marry, I will marry,
I will marry you!

(A) Ah ha ha, now I see,
You love my money but
you don't love me,
So I won't marry,
I won't marry,
I won't marry you!

10

Can you speak more than one language at the same time? Aunty Joyce can! Most Anglo-Indians can speak both English and the state language. After many years of speaking two or more languages, they now have their own way of talking. Here are some words and phrases to liven up your next conversation.

'How do you do?'
'Fine, thank you,
just like
a ladoo,
one paise two.'

———————

The next time someone asks how you're doing, you can respond this way. In years gone by, you could buy two 'fine' ladoos for 1 paisa.

chutney
mary
Someone who's dressed in a very silly manner

———————

'You can't go to the party like that. You look like a Chutney Mary.'

old fish in
a rubber dish
To act or look older than your age

———————

'That dress makes baby Betty look like an old fish in a rubber dish!'

'Thank you very much.'
'You're welcome,

magarmach.'

**A comical way
to thank someone**

fell from heaven
in a bread basket

**Extremely
innocent**

'Aunty Judy
could never tell
a lie. She fell
from heaven in
a bread basket.'

monkey on
hot bricks

**Someone who
can't sit still**

'Even in church,
Tom is like a
monkey on
hot bricks.'

charlie boy,
budi girl,
it's time for bed!

**'Charlie boy' and
'budi girl' is what
you call a younger
boy and girl respectively.**

Most Anglo-Indians follow the Christian faith and the church is their place of worship.

On Sundays, Uncle Charlie and Aunty Joyce attend church where they sing in the choir and people sing along. Meanwhile, Rosie and Leslie attend Sunday school, where they sing, play, colour and listen to stories from the Bible. The Bible is their holy book.

Christians believe in one God and that he came to this world in human form as Jesus. They believe that God's greatest commandment is agape love. This kind of love is unearned. From a young age, Leslie and Rosie were told that love is best utilized when it is given away, so they were taught to be kind and caring towards everybody around them. This includes people that don't look or dress like them, people who are less fortunate than them and even those who are not always kind to them.

BIBLE

HOLY bOOK

cross

I'm sure you've heard of a family tree, but have you heard of a fruit of the Spirit tree?

The Lovedale family has a poster of this tree up on their wall. This tree stands as a reminder of the nine fruits of the spirit.

Mentioned in the Bible, these fruits are qualities that people are encouraged to have. Can you think of some more special fruits that you can add to this tree and practise in your daily life? Write them in the blanks on the opposite page.

love • joy • peace • _____
• patience • kindness _____
• goodness • gentleness • _____
faithfulness • _____
• self-control • _____

16

Christmas is a major Anglo-Indian festival, celebrating the birth of Jesus. The word 'Christmas' comes from the words 'Christ' (saviour) and 'mass' (gathering), which together mean a gathering to honour the Christ.

Christmas is Rosie and Leslie's favourite time of the year.

In the days leading up to it, they help Uncle Charlie decorate the tree by hanging ornaments on it. Penny-the-Pom helps too by running around the tree in circles along with the fairy lights.

Aunty Joyce takes the children to the dry fruit market to buy ingredients for her famous Christmas fruit cake. Christmas cake is a long-standing tradition among Anglo-Indian families. Its smell alone makes you feel warm and cosy.

Join in the Christmas preparations by making these fried sweet treats with the help of an adult.

KULKULS

ingredients

1 egg
2 cups flour
¼ cup semolina
A pinch of baking soda
2 tbsp butter, ghee or oil
½ tbsp vanilla essence
½ cup water
¼ cup sugar
Oil or ghee, for frying
Icing sugar, cinnamon powder
    and nutmeg powder, for dusting

preparation

① **You can, with the help of an adult**, combine all the ingredients in a big mixing bowl to form a dough and knead it until smooth.

② **You can** divide the dough into equal marble-sized pieces.

3. Now **you can** spread and press down each ball of dough on to the tines of a fork. It will take on the fork's striped impression. Then roll the long piece of dough into a curl and off the fork. Repeat this process with each piece of dough.

4. **Ask an adult** to help you deep-fry them in oil or ghee until golden brown.

ready!!

Dunk the kulkuls into a container with icing sugar, cinnamon powder and nutmeg powder. Shake, swirl and make a joyful noise!

PS: The little swirls are meant to represent a striped Jewish swaddling cloth that baby Jesus was probably wrapped in at birth.

The other big festival that the Anglo-Indians celebrate is easter. In Christianity, this is the day that Jesus came back to life after his death, and so it is observed as the festival of new life and new beginnings.

Did you know that most decorations used during both these festivals have a symbolic meaning? Learn about them while exploring some Christmas and Easter craft ideas. You can make these ornaments yourself and celebrate DIY-style.

materials

Sheets of art paper
Pencil, glue, scissors
** and paper punch**
Crayons, beads and glitter
1½ metres of string or ribbon

instructions

1. Trace the shapes on to the art paper.

2. For the Christmas ornaments (Tree, Candy Cane, Star and Wreath), punch a hole in the circle marked.

3. Pull a 5-inch-long string or ribbon through each hole. Tie the two ends together to form a loop.

4. For the Easter Lilies and Easter Eggs, paste the decorated shapes on to a long string or ribbon and make your own bunting.

5. Hang the decorations on a Christmas tree or around the house.

christmas tree

A Christmas tree that is evergreen, which means its leaves will never fade or fall, symbolizes God's ever fresh and unfading love for us.

easter eggs

An egg reminds us of birth and life. It is the start of something new!

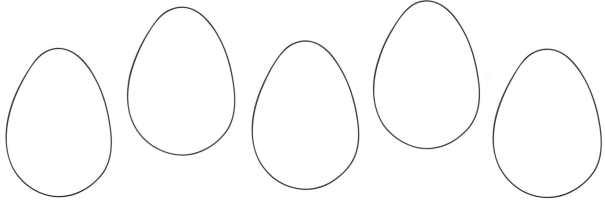

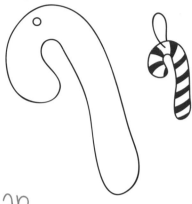

candy cane

This symbolizes the staff that the shepherds carry. Both kings and shepherds were present on the first Christmas Day.

star

Stars at Christmas time represent the Star of Bethlehem. This iconic star led the kings from the East to baby Jesus in the manger.

wreath

This is usually made from holly leaves in a circular shape. A circle has no end, and so a wreath reminds us of God's unending love for us.

easter lilies

They represent purity and hope as they lie dormant in the ground all year round but bloom around Easter time without fail. The lilies are native to Japan, but were brought to England in the 1700s–1800s. Today, they can be found everywhere in the world.

The kids also pitch in to help Aunty Joyce prepare Christmas treats like rose cookies, sugar cookies, kulkuls and guava cheese. Penny-the-Pom loves licking the leftover batter!

In the evenings, the whole family sits around the piano with cups of hot chocolate and sings Christmas carols.

fruit cake

keema chops

kedgeree

mulligatawny soup

rose cookies

yellow rice and ball curry

On other festivals, birthdays and anniversaries, the Lovedales prepare unique Anglo-Indian recipes, which are a combination of both Indian and British cuisines.

They make delicious dishes like mulligatawny soup, kedgeree, vindaloo, jalfrezi, glazie and keema chops. Penny-the-Pom loves yellow rice and ball curry!

Perfect as party appetizers, this Anglo-Indian breakfast dish is easy to make, healthy and super yummy!

devilled eggs/ avocados

ingredients

**2 hard-boiled eggs
   or 3 avocados
1 tsp kasundi (or mustard sauce)
1 tbsp mayonnaise
A pinch of chilli powder
A pinch of salt
Equipment: 1 piping bag**

preparation

1. **Ask an adult** to help you slice the eggs or avocados lengthwise in half and carefully remove the yolks or pits.

2. **You can** place all the yolks (or two avocado halves) on a plate. Using a fork, mash mash mash till you have a smooth paste.

3 **You can** add kasundi, mayonnaise, chilli powder and salt to the mixture. Make sure you blend them all until smooth.

4 **Ask an adult** to help you fill a piping bag with the mixture. **You can** now pipe it into the egg white halves or remaining avocado halves.

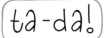

ta-da!

Your devilled eggs or avocados are ready. Chomp away!

Many Anglo-Indian weddings take place during the winter season in India. Rosie and Leslie are especially excited about one such wedding, Aunty Sheryl's, in which they get to play an important role.

Aunty Sheryl is having a Christian ceremony at the cathedral. She'll be wearing a beautiful white dress fit for a queen and her husband-to-be will wear a black tuxedo.

The ceremony begins with flower girls in pretty little dresses walking ahead of the bride. They carry a basket of flower petals, which they shower along the path as they walk. Then comes a pageboy, who carries the wedding rings that the couple will exchange during the ceremony.

The bride and her father walk down to the front of the church where the groom stands, waiting for his wife-to-be.

At Aunty Sheryl's wedding, Rosie and Leslie are going to be the flower girl and pageboy respectively. But you can't just walk down the aisle in any ole manner—there's a special step that you need to do.

It's known as the

hesitation step.

Rosie and Leslie have been practising this step at home so that they get it just right on the wedding day. You can try it with them now.

It goes like this: right step, left hesitate; left step, right hesitate. The hesitation step is used during other formal ceremonies as well such as graduations.

Walking down the aisle in this manner ensures that you don't have to rush. This way you can do your duty properly, be it sprinkling flower petals or carrying the rings very carefully.

After the ceremony, the couple along with their guests revel with a dinner and dance party. These parties are lively and full of interesting traditions.

unity ceremony

The couple takes two things that are separate at first—two candles or two jars of sand—and combines them. The candles are used together to light another candle, and the sand from both jars is poured into a single jar.

Do you think it's possible to sort the grains back into their original jars? Is it possible to tell which part of the flame came from which candle? No! This is what it means to be a family. Separate people come together to form one family. That's how

Aunty Joyce and Uncle Charlie started out and now along with Rosie, Leslie and Penny-the-Pom, the five of them can't be separated! Can you think of other elements that once mixed can't be unmixed?

bouquet toss

At some point during the dinner party, the bride's unmarried female friends gather around her. The bride then closes her eyes and tosses her bridal bouquet over to them. Tradition has it that whoever catches it will get married next!

farewell arch

At the end of the party, the guests hold hands to form a human arch leading to the exit. You can think of it as a very long arch that is formed while playing Oranges and Lemons or Posham Pa. The bride and groom pass through the arch collecting hugs, kisses and blessings from each guest on their way out. After this creative farewell, the couple leave with a smile on their faces.

34

The Lovedale family enjoys going to the country club. Leslie and Rosie are learning horse riding and lawn tennis at the club.

When the British were in India, they set up various recreational and sporting country clubs in various cities. These clubs used to be exclusively for the British families living in India, and later they were opened up to Anglo-Indians and Indians.

These usually have a clubhouse with grand colonial architecture that speak of an era gone by. Many country clubs still have the tradition of strict formal or sporting attire.

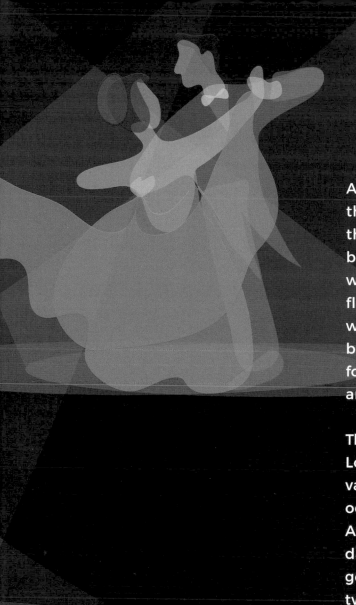

Aunty Joyce tells her children that when she was young, the clubs used to host formal ballroom dances, where the women would wear beautiful flowing gowns and the men would dress in tailcoats and bow ties. They danced the foxtrot, the waltz, the cha-cha and the jive!

The country club that the Lovedales go to still hosts various dances on special occasions. Uncle Charlie and Aunty Joyce are excellent dancers. They're exceptionally good at the Charleston, the twist and the jive.

Leslie and Rosie are learning some of the dance steps from Aunty Joyce and Uncle Charlie. You can learn along with them too! Here's a fun dance to do when you don't have a lot of space around you. It's called the hand jive and it involves various hand movements, bumps and claps.

The whole routine lasts for two sets of eight beats and you can repeat it as long as the music lasts. Let's count it together. Here we go!

1 tap
tap 2

³ clap
clap ₄

⁵ swipe
swipe
₆

⁷
swipe
swipe ₈

¹ bump
bump ₂

³ bump
bump ₄

⁵ hitch
-hike ₆

⁷ hitch
-hike ₈

Being exposed to both the Indian and British cultures have made the Anglo-Indians extremely versatile, with many of them leaving their mark on the world. Here's a list of some iconic anglo-indians.

ruskin bond

A much-loved children's author, **Ruskin Bond** has been awarded the Padma Shri and Padma Bhushan for his contributions to Indian literature. Characters like Rusty in *The Room on the Roof* and Binya in *The Blue Umbrella* live in the hearts and on the shelves of every Indian family.

Educationist, quizmaster and motivational speaker, **Barry O'Brien** was nominated by the governor of West Bengal to the West Bengal Legislative Assembly to represent the Anglo-Indian community. He is also the president-in-chief of the All-India Anglo-Indian Association.

barry o'brien

Anna Leonowens was an educator, travel writer and social activist. Her experiences of teaching the children of the King of Siam (now Thailand) inspired the book *Anna and the King of Siam* by Margaret Landon.

An internationally renowned singer, **Engelbert Humperdinck** has won a Golden Globe Award and has his very own star on the Hollywood Walk of Fame. Some of his evergreen classics are 'Release Me', 'The Last Waltz' and 'Quando Quando Quando'.

Helen Ann Richardson Khan, popularly known as Helen, is a prominent actress-dancer in the Hindi film industry. She has over 700 films, two Filmfare Awards and the Padma Shri to her name.

A stand-up comedian famous for his hilarious observations, **Russell Peters** is also a film actor and producer. His live shows at locations like Mumbai's NSCI Stadium, Toronto's Scotiabank Arena and The O2 Arena in London have always been sold out!

Leslie Claudius was part of the Indian field hockey team and won three Olympic gold medals (1948, 1952, 1956) and one silver medal (1960). He was honoured with the Padma Shri and mentioned in the Guinness World Records.

Derek O'Brien is a Rajya Sabha Member of Parliament, a television personality and quizmaster. He is fondly associated with the Bournvita Quiz Contest that made its way on to television sets every Sunday morning in the 1990s.

frank anthony

Frank Anthony was the founder-chairman of the trust that runs several schools named after him. These schools are spread across New Delhi, Bengaluru and Kolkata. He was a representative of the Anglo-Indian community in the Indian Parliament.

Diana Hayden is an actress and model. In 1997, she won the Miss World contest and became the third Indian contestant to have received the Miss World title. She has acted in several films, including a version of Shakespeare's *Othello*.

diana hayden

acknowledgements

A heartful of gratitude to Sohini Mitra, Arpita Nath, Aditi Batra, Antra K and the entire team at Penguin Random House India for their tireless efforts in making this book possible.

A special thank you to Mayura Misra who is truly a crusader for reading.

Last but not least, much appreciation is due to my family and friends who have cheered me on—foremost of them being my best friend and husband, Jamshed Madan.

READ MORE IN THE SERIES

Have You Met the Parsis?